Linked up

The Ultimate LinkedIn®
Job Search Guide

Chris Perry

LinkedUp: The Ultimate LinkedIn® Job Search Guide

Chris Perry
Brand & Marketing Generator
http://www.chrisperry.me

For ordering information or special discounts for bulk purchases, please contact Chris Perry at *careerrocketeer@gmail.com*.

TABLE OF CONTENTS

- Optimize Your Profile
  You will learn all of the components needed for an optimal LinkedIn profile that will serve as the launchpad for all of your personal branding and career search efforts.

- Build Your Network & Your Credibility
  You will learn about how to use LinkedIn to increase your network connections, as well as how to network your personal brand and increase your credibility within your target industry or audience.

- Find Your Job
  You will learn some ways you can leverage LinkedIn's features to identify and effectively pursue target job opportunities.

INTRODUCTION

Networking is one of the most important -- if not the most important -- activity that you can leverage throughout your career.

Because the majority of job opportunities are not publicly advertised, it becomes vital that you manage and grow your network of career stakeholders to ensure a healthy flow of support, information and potential job leads.

In today's digital age, while in-person networking will always be important, many first impressions begin with an online search, making it even more essential that you be present, searchable and branded in everything you do online.

SO, WHY START WITH LINKEDIN?

- LinkedIn is an interconnected network of over 120 million professionals (and growing) from around the world, representing 150 industries and 200 countries.

- LinkedIn is highly ranked in Google and other search engines, and your LinkedIn profile is often in the top search results for your name.

- Your LinkedIn profile is your online resume. Not only does your profile require your experience, education and credentials for 100% completion, but it is also where career stakeholders expect to find you and your professional information.

- Your network of contacts is one of the most valuable assets you have to leverage throughout your career. While similar to other top social networking sites, LinkedIn is specifically designed to help you manage your professional network for your career and/or your business.

- LinkedIn has many other features that can help you build your credibility and personal brand online, network with potential business partners, customers and employers, and find and apply for new career opportunities.

WHAT ARE THE NEXT STEPS?

Whether you're already active on LinkedIn or have yet to get started, this guide will teach you the essentials to leveraging LinkedIn for career success, including how to:

1. **Optimize Your Profile:** You will learn all of the components needed for an optimal LinkedIn profile that will serve as the launchpad for all of your personal branding and career search efforts.

2. **Build Your Network & Credibility:** You will learn about how to use LinkedIn to increase your network connections, as well as how to network your personal brand and increase your credibility within your target industry or audience.

3. **Find Your Job:** You will learn some ways you can leverage LinkedIn's features to identify and effectively pursue target job opportunities.

CHAPTER 1:
Optimize Your Profile

OPTIMIZE YOUR PROFILE

After signing up on LinkedIn, the best way to get started is to complete your profile.

This is easy to do, and LinkedIn makes it even easier by walking you through a step-by-step process to a 100% complete professional profile.

A 100% COMPLETE PROFILE REQUIRES:

- Adding your current position (25%)
- Adding a past or current position (15%)
- Adding another past or current position (15%)
- Adding your education (15%)
- Adding your profile summary (5%)
- Adding a profile photo (5%)
- Adding your specialties (5%)
- Asking for recommendation #1 (5%)
- Asking for recommendation #2 (5%)
- Asking for recommendation #3 (5%)

Completing your profile (as outlined above) is the first step towards optimizing your presence on LinkedIn.

However, it is strongly recommended that you fill out and enhance your profile above and beyond what LinkedIn suggests.

HOW DO YOU ENHANCE YOUR PROFILE?

Name: Include your full name as you would like to be known professionally; however, don't forget to include a nickname or maiden name, as this will make it easier for all potential contacts to find and connect with you no matter how they know you.

5

Identifying your personal brand may take some time, but it is worth the thought and investment.

Getting Started:

1. Write down your unique strengths (those you feel make you stand out from the rest)

2. Ask your friends, family and colleagues to do the same

3. Identify the top 3 to 5 overlapping strengths that you feel will support the career direction you want to pursue

4. Now that you have your strengths, create/find a word or phrase that can become your personal brand and that represents these strengths

5. Develop a short elevator pitch that can follow your brand, describing your strengths (i.e. your value) in more detail

Be sure to feature your personal brand in your Profile Header and both your brand and your supporting pitch in your Summary.

Photo: Select a profile photo that is both professional and consistent with other online profiles you may have and maintain, as this helps put a name to a face and makes you more recognizable across networks.

Profile Header: While this automatically defaults to your current position, this is what people see first and associate with you. Therefore, don't just leave it as your current position and don't make it something too general like "Student" or "Marketing Professional." This is the ideal place to promote your personal brand and other more attention-grabbing titles.

Locale: This identifies where you work and makes you more searchable by a specific geography.

Industry: This identifies what you do (*or more importantly what you want to do*) and makes you better searchable on LinkedIn by chosen industry.

Recommendations: Ask for recommendations from as many contacts as possible. Remember, they don't have to be long. Brief recommendations are just as valuable as longer ones, especially on an online profile. You may want to offer to write each recommender one in return, when appropriate.

Websites: You can add up to 3 links from your profile to promote your company, personal website, blog, other online profiles and more.

Public Profile: Choose which parts of your profile are visible to others so they can find you. Also, don't forget to customize your own profile URL to use in your email signature, on your business cards, etc. This will make your profile easier to remember in your career and business networking.

Status Updates: Your status updates are visible to your entire network, offering you a way to share your activity with them. You may share a link to a great article or resource, an opportunity you know of or

6

even your own job candidacy and career goals. Just ensure your status updates support your personal brand and don't come across too self-promotional.

Summary: This is ideal for a brief professional overview of your experience and a personal branding statement. Include keywords and phrases to optimize your searchability.

Specialties: Include a few specific skills or experiences you consider your professional specialties. It's best to list these in bullet form for better legibility. Again, add keywords and phrases to optimize your searchability.

Experience: Include as much of your current and past work history as appropriate for your desired career path. Highlight your key accomplishments from each position and quantify as many as possible to enhance your value proposition. Also, optimize your descriptions with keywords and phrases.

Education: Feature your education and any academic activities, clubs, etc. in which you were active.

Additional Information: This features your site links, your interests, your honors and groups.

Personal Information: Include any personal and contact details that you feel comfortable making public for people to get in touch with you.

Contact Preferences: These are important to include as they let your profile viewers know what they can contact you for, including career opportunities, business ventures, expertise requests and more.

ADVANCED FEATURES

There are a number of more advanced features that you can apply to your profile to bring it to life.

Sections: There are several sections you can include and fill out on your profile to organize and feature your skills, accomplishments and involvement, including:

- Publications
- Certifications
- Courses
- Honors and Awards
- Languages
- Organizations
- Projects
- Patents
- Test Scores

Twitter: Sync Twitter with LinkedIn and make your Twitter account visible on your profile. You can also have your status updated with your latest tweets to cross-promote your Twitter activity.

Groups: When you join LinkedIn Groups, you can choose to display their logos on your profile for others to see. *Read Chapter 2 and Chapter 3 to learn more about how to use Groups to build your network and find job opportunities.*

Skills: Skills is a part of the LinkedIn search engine where you can search specific skills to determine their popularity, review featured professionals, companies and locations associated with that skill, find related jobs and networking groups, as well as learn whether that particular skill is trending up or down. *Read Chapter 3 to learn more about how to use Skills to build your brand and find jobs opportunities.*

Applications: There are many apps, all free, that you can add to your profile, including:

1. *Wordpress & Blog Link:* Feed your blog posts or the posts from your favorite blog right into your profile.

2. *Google, SlideShare & Box.net:* Embed and share files and presentations with others in a portfolio on your LinkedIn Profile.

3. *Reading List by Amazon:* Feature your own works or your favorite or recommended reads for others.

4. *My Travel:* Share your upcoming trips, current location, and travel stats with your network via TripIt.

5. *Polls:* Collect actionable data from your connections to use for your career, business and/or even your job search.

Check out the entire Applications list on LinkedIn for additional apps with which you can enhance your profile.

CHAPTER 2:
Build Your Network
& Your Credibility

BUILD YOUR NETWORK & YOUR CREDIBILITY

Now that you have your profile in order, it's time to start building your network and establishing credibility for you and your personal brand.

However, before you can build your credibility, you need a network in which to build it.

TYPES OF CONNECTIONS:

Here are some key definitions to help you get started:

1st degree LinkedIn connections are your direct connections who you have either invited to connect or who have invited you to connect.

2nd degree LinkedIn connections are people who are directly connected to your first degree connections but not directly connected to you.

3rd degree LinkedIn connections are people who are directly connected to your second degree connections.

Group Member connections are people who are none of the above, but who are members of the same LinkedIn Group(s).

MAKING CONNECTIONS:

The best way to start building your network is to import to LinkedIn your contacts from other programs and address books.

13

You can also search for your contacts to invite to connect using the search and/or advanced search functions.

Once you have identified an individual with whom you want to connect, you can send them invitations if you know their email addresses and/or if you both currently or previously worked and/or studied together.

You don't have to connect with someone to contact them. However, if *Send message* is not an option on someone's profile and you don't know the person's email address and you were not a colleague or classmate in the past, then you have two additional ways to get in contact with them.

You can do this by using either the **Introduction** or the **InMail** feature.

1. **Introduction:** The Introduction feature is free to all users. On your 2nd and 3rd degree connections' profiles, you will see a link *Get introduced through a Connection*. This takes you to a *Request an Introduction* page where you can enter your message and send it through the chain of people between you and that person.

2. **InMail:** InMails are private messages that enable you to contact or be directly contacted by another LinkedIn user. InMail is a paid feature that can be purchased individually or as part of a premium LinkedIn account.

JOINING GROUPS:

LinkedIn Groups are member-created communities for just about any industry, profession or area of interest you can imagine.

NOTE

When you identify someone with whom you want to connect, make sure this individual knows you.

If not, they may reject the invitation and select *I Don't Know This User*.

If you accrue too many of these rejected invitations, LinkedIn will restrict you from sending invitations to others in the future, limiting your networking opportunities.

They are free to join, and you can be a member of up to 50 groups from the over one million groups (and growing) available. Many groups are open to everyone, but there are some that require approval by the group's manager in order to join.

Once you join a group, you can immediately start networking by getting involved in group discussions.

Every group has a discussion board. This is a great place for you to learn new information, engage in a conversation with someone new and contribute your own insights and ideas.

The more value you can contribute to the group, the more professional and credible you will come across to your fellow group members. This will help you advance your personal brand in your target groups and networks.

Many groups also have created subgroups that are more niche or geography-focused that you can join.

STARTING GROUPS:

In addition to joining LinkedIn Groups, you may also choose to start your own group.

Because there are already over one million groups (and growing) on LinkedIn, it isn't easy to grow membership in a new group unless you already have an association, club or group offline (or online) that you can invite to join, or unless you choose to start a group within a new or untapped niche area that is becoming increasingly popular.

Another option for group leadership is to become an active and credible contributor in a couple target groups and then reach out to the owner about opportunities to become a manager or moderator.

EXPERT TIP

Joining groups allows you to directly contact fellow group members depending on their privacy settings.

This can make it easier to reach out to potential contacts and employers outside your network.

NOTE

Be mindful of any group rules which are usually posted as featured discussions in each group so that you don't break any unknowingly.

This allows you to help lead a group and build your credibility within your industry or area of interest without having to build a group from scratch.

Whether you start groups or simply join them, LinkedIn Groups are an invaluable way to network your brand and make career connections.

OPEN NETWORKING:

Many professionals do not start with a large network of 1st degree or 2nd degree contacts within their chosen industry and as a result, they find it more challenging to reach out to new contacts and career stakeholders. Open networking is the process of connecting with professionals you do not already know for mutual benefit and network expansion.

By open networking with other professionals, you gain more 1st degree connections and in turn, you gain access to message them and their connections, some of whom may be target hiring managers, employers and recruiters.

So, how do you start open networking? Many open networkers note their open networking status in their profile headers and summaries and openly invite requests to connect. You can also search the LinkedIn Groups directory for "open networking" or "open networkers" and join open networking groups on LinkedIn.

Some of the more popular groups have their own websites where you can learn more, including:

- TopLinked.com
- OpenNetworker.com
- LION500.com
- InvitesWelcome.com

16

ANSWERS:

Answers is a unique Q&A forum on LinkedIn that allows members to post their own questions by category, as well as contribute answers to others' questions.

Getting involved in asking questions, answering questions and sharing insights and ideas related to your chosen industry is another effective way to establish your personal brand in an area of expertise. This is also a great way to identify potential new connections and build a network full of potential career stakeholders who now know of you because of your value and your contributions.

EXPERT TIP

The person who posts each question must select the best answers from those who respond. If yours is selected, it is shown on your profile as sort of a badge of expertise on a given topic or given industry.

EVENTS:

LinkedIn also has an increasingly popular events calendar that may become helpful in your personal branding and career search efforts.

You can search events by keyword, date and place. Once you have your search results, you can sign up to attend any events that pique your interest, as well as see who out of your connections is attending.

Events, whether online or in-person, can do a number of things to help you in your career:

1. They can provide new information and skills training that you can apply to your own current career or entrepreneurial work.

2. They can serve as continuing education and industry-related activity to feature on your resume and in your interviews as signs of your involvement in the industry.

EXPERT TIP

You can promote your own created events directly to your network or target contacts, which can help position you as a job candidate with experience and expertise that could help solve some of their business challenges.

3. They can provide you an opportunity to meet new like-minded connections and build your network.

Also, hosting/creating your own events is very easy to do on LinkedIn Events and can also be a great way to build your own brand as a thought leader in your industry.

CHAPTER 3:
Find Your Job

FIND YOUR JOB

As explained in the previous chapters, LinkedIn is a powerful tool for long-term personal branding and career and business networking.

However, it also offers a number of features to help you in your more short-term job search process.

JOBS:

One of the best features on LinkedIn is its own built-in job board.

You can instantly search jobs by keyword, job title or company name, or you can use the advanced search feature to filter jobs by other criteria, including company size, geography and your level of connection to the company's employees.

On the main jobs page, LinkedIn will also make relevant suggestions to you based on your profile content and completeness.

For some jobs, you will be able to apply directly on the LinkedIn site. You will be asked to submit a cover letter and/or a resume.

For other jobs, companies may route you to their career page or company job board in order to continue the application process.

For any given job in your search results, you not only can see the recruiter who posted the job, but can see which of your connections currently work for the company and can then identify who might be able to refer you to this recruiter as a candidate for the position in question.

> **FACT**
>
> When you apply on LinkedIn, the recruiter will not only be able to access your resume and cover letter, but will also be able to immediately click through to your profile.
>
> This makes it imperative that your profile be 100% complete and branded so to make the best first impression possible.
>
> While a 100% complete profile requires 3 recommendations, the more you can obtain from your network connections, the more endorsed you will come across to recruiters and hiring managers.

In addition, each job posting will offer links to similar jobs and to jobs that viewers of this specific job also viewed. This is a great way to uncover related postings that may have been missed in your previous searches.

COMPANIES:

Another useful resource for your job search is Companies, LinkedIn's company directory.

It is very comprehensive as it is constantly updated by LinkedIn members as they complete their profiles with their current and previous employers.

You can use the search functions to filter by name, industry and geography, and you can see where the companies are headquartered both nationally and globally, as well as how many employees they have.

For some companies, LinkedIn includes helpful information, including average tenure of employees at the company, the company's male-to-female ratio, the average age of employees, and more.

Not only does this directory help you identify new companies that you may not have already targeted, but it also tells you if you have a 1st or 2nd degree contact in the company, as well as whether the company has any job listings currently posted on LinkedIn Jobs.

PROFILE:

Beyond completing your profile 100%, you can also leverage your Status Updates, Summary, Specialties and Experience and Applications to promote your candidacy for a new opportunity.

Your status updates will be visible to all of your network connections, so be sure that your job search can be public knowledge. Don't forget to check the status updates of your connections and target hiring managers and recruiters, as some people will post job openings there.

As mentioned in *Chapter 1*, completing your Summary, Specialties and Experience sections with key accomplishments, strengths and skills and optimizing them with the right keywords and phrases will not only better communicate your personal brand and value proposition to an organization, but can also help you get found more often by target career stakeholders and may help generate more outreach from employers and recruiters.

You may also use some applications to enhance your job search. For example, you can use *Box.net* to share your resume, bio and/or cover letter for download and *SlideShare* to feature a presentation on why an employer should hire you.

GROUPS:

There are a number of ways to leverage your LinkedIn groups in your job search.

1. **Group Membership:** Membership in and contribution to an industry or specific employer's group helps create that first commonality with recruiters and hiring managers and makes it easier for you to reach out to them and vice versa. It may also give you additional insight into what the industry or company is doing, whether they are hiring, and what you can do to contribute value and fulfill their needs. Also be sure to search your group memberships for "Recruiter" to help you identify recruiters specializing in your target industry or functional area.

2. **Discussions:** A number of jobs are posted on different group discussion boards which provide you leads for opportunities not posted on LinkedIn Jobs. You can also post your candidacy as a discussion if the group rules allow for it. You may also see a discussion that identifies an individual or company's problem that your expertise can solve in a potential new position or consulting gig.

3. **Jobs:** Each group owner or manager can choose to feed specific jobs targeted to his or her membership from the LinkedIn Jobs database into their Jobs section. This may help save you some time by providing you postings already filtered for your industry, function etc.

4. **Digest Email:** For each of the groups you join, you can access a Group Settings page. Be sure to activate your Digest Email, mailed either daily or weekly, as it will provide you with the latest group discussions, career tips and job leads so you never miss key advice and opportunities.

While you should create your own customized list of up to 50 groups to join, here are 10 career search group recommendations to get you started:

1. *Career Rocketeer*
2. *Star:Performer Career Network*
3. *Hiring for Hope*
4. *Personal Branding Network*
5. *Career Central*
6. *CareerLink*
7. *Your Graduate School Alumni Group*
8. *Your College Alumni Group*
9. *Your Past Employer's LinkedIn Group*
10. *Your Target Industry Group*

NETWORKING:

It is also important to network with others, as there are many "hidden" jobs that haven't been posted anywhere that might be a good match if only you can network in-person or one-on-one with the right person. You may not know all of the right people, so that is where your current network can play a role.

As mentioned in *Chapter 2*, if you identify a person with whom you would like to connect about a specific opportunity or opportunities in general at a specific company, you can try to reach out directly to them in a number of ways:

- **Email:** If you know the person's email, you can reach out to them. If you don't know the person's email, you can either try to figure it out or move on to the next options.

- **Send Message:** The *Send message* is a direct way to connect with a target contact. It is not an option on everyone's profile, as this depends on what level of connection you have with them and/or their privacy settings.

- **Introduction:** The Introduction feature is free to all users. On your 2nd and 3rd degree connections' profiles, you will see a link *Get introduced through a Connection*. This takes you to a *Request an Introduction* page where you can enter your message and send it through the chain of people between you and that person. This is how you can leverage your current network to your advantage.

- **InMail:** InMails are private messages that enable you to contact or be directly contacted by another LinkedIn user. InMail is a paid feature that can be purchased individually or as part of a premium account.

EXPERT TIP

Most companies' email addresses are the same as their domain name (*ex. @abc.com and www.abc.com*).

Therefore, if you do a quick Google search of "@abc.com," you can usually find others' email addresses from the company and determine the name format typically used (*ex. jsmith@abc.com or john.smith@abc.com*).

Once you know how you will reach these contacts, you can reach out to them for informational interviews.

OPEN NETWORKING:

As mentioned in *Chapter 2*, open networking is the process of connecting with professionals you do not already know for mutual benefit and network expansion.

By open networking with other professionals, you gain more 1st degree connections and in turn, you gain access to message them and their connections, some of whom may be target hiring managers, employers and recruiters.

Many open networkers note their open networking status in their profile headers and summaries and openly invite requests to connect.

You can also search the LinkedIn Groups directory for "open networking" or "open networkers" and join open networking groups on LinkedIn. Some of the more popular groups have their own websites where you can learn more, including:

- TopLinked.com
- OpenNetworker.com
- LION500.com
- InvitesWelcome.com

There are also several job search-specific open networking groups that will come up when you do a Groups directory search.

If you want a list of the top job and career open networking groups organized by location, profession and industry, visit TopJobGroups.com.

INFORMATIONAL INTERVIEWS:

Informational interviews have a number of things going against them. They sound boring, ineffective and hard to get.

However, if used correctly, an informational interview can make or break your job search. They work because they allow you to make a personal connection with a real human being who is typically in a much better position to endorse you and recommend you internally in his/her company.

How to Get Informational Interviews:

Here are some points to remember when requesting an informational interview:

- Proofread your message for GRAMMAR
- Hook them with a subject line that is personalized
- Briefly introduce yourself and your brand
- Leverage any commonalities you might have
- They know you want a job, so don't ask for one
- Don't forget your contact information

Here is a true-life informational interview request example that had a very high response rate:

Subject: *John - Career Question*

Body: *Dear Mr. John Smith,*

My name is Chris Perry, and I work currently in brand management in Parsippany, NJ. I am pursuing a long-term career in marketing and specifically career opportunities at COMPANY NAME.

I am interested in speaking with you about your career, COMPANY NAME's culture and your marketing team's various programs and activities.

> ### EXPERT TIP
>
> In addition to not requesting a job upfront, do not send your resume to the interviewees unless they request it.
>
> Sending your resume looks presumptuous and makes your call seem like it's all about you, when the interview needs to be all about them.

Would you be willing to set up a short 30-minute informational interview with me in the coming week or two during which I could learn more about your career in marketing and your company?

I truly appreciate your time and your consideration.

I look forward to hearing from you soon!

Sincerely,

Chris Perry
Email Address - Cell: Phone Number

How to Make the Most of Informational Interviews:

Here are some points to remember when conducting an informational interview:

- Be on time and respectful of their time
- Be prepared with intelligent questions
- Don't ask for a job, but do mention that you have applied for a specific opportunity at the company if it is true
- Ask them how they broke into their careers and if they have any advice on how to break into one in the company
- Ask for referrals within the company
- Offer some ideas, if appropriate, to show that you're creative and invested in their company and/or projects
- Offer to help them if appropriate
- Send a follow-up thank you note/email
- Follow up with them periodically to keep yourself top-of-mind for future opportunities that come up or that you apply for

Informational interviews will increase your chances of finding and being considered for jobs, especially the "hidden" ones (Only 20% of jobs openings are publicly posted).

You should also consider doing these periodically even while you have a job just to continue building your network and keeping in shape for future job searches.

SKILLS:

As mentioned in *Chapter 1*, Skills is a part of the LinkedIn search engine where you can search specific skills to determine their popularity, review featured professionals, companies and locations associated with that skill, find related jobs and networking groups, as well as learn whether that particular skill is trending up or down.

You can start by selecting *Skills* from the drop-down menu under *More* on the main navigation bar. Search a skill, such as Digital Marketing, Adobe Software or Budgeting, and you'll be brought to that specific skill's homepage.

You can see if this skill is on an upward trend and see its growth and popularity versus other related skills. Viewing its growth alongside related skills is a good measure for determining new skills you may want to develop to become more marketable.

You can browse the top related companies associated with the skill and follow them to keep tabs on who they're hiring, company news or newly-posted job openings.

The related locations section will tell you where that skill is most in-demand, if relocation for a new position is an option for you. This may help you focus or refocus your search efforts in a new city or region.

You can also browse the groups section to find new groups associated with that skill in which you can start contributing and branding yourself as an expert in that skill.

There are two ways you can add a skill to your profile:

EXPERT TIP

Skills not only lets you add the top, in-demand skills to your profile in your Skills section, improving your searchability within the Skills database, but is a powerful tool for identifying and optimizing the keywords you use in your profile in addition to those you identified using job postings.

By searching a specific skill, you can see whether it is the most popular wording for that strength or expertise. You can also see other related skills and compare their relative growth.

While you definitely want to include the most popular Skills and keywords in your profile, you may also want to choose some that are less popular, as that may help you stand out as a bigger fish in a smaller pond.

29

1. Click the *Add Sections* link on your profile and select the Skills you want to include

2. Visit that specific skill's homepage and add it manually

JOBS INSIDER:

Jobs Insider is a free LinkedIn job search toolbar application that you can download as part of your Internet Explorer or Firefox internet browser.

Jobs Insider allows you to see your inside connections for online job postings. Here's how it works:

- Open any job posting on Monster.com, CareerBuilder.com, Craigslist.org, SimplyHired.com, Dice.com, or Vault.com

- Jobs Insider shows you the people in your network that work at the hiring company

- Request an introduction to the hiring manager, get your resume to the right inside contact and/or learn more about the company

To download Jobs Insider for your job search, do a quick Google search for "LinkedIn Jobs Insider".

PREMIUM ACCOUNTS:

There is always a question about whether to upgrade one's free LinkedIn account to one of the premium paid accounts.

LinkedIn offers three different types of premium accounts, including Business, Job Seeker and Talent Seeker accounts. You can find these by clicking *Upgrade My Account* under *More* on the main navigation bar. Each premium account type offers three different levels with varying benefits and features for different annual and monthly prices.

Naturally, the two that may make the most sense for you would be the Business account, if you're an entrepreneur or current career professional building your brand and network, or the Job Seeker account, if you're currently in the market for a new opportunity.

Selected Business Account Features:

- See more profiles and expanded profile details in every people search you conduct
- Get introduced to target companies
- See exactly who has viewed your profile
- InMail messaging opportunities
- Let anyone message you for free with OpenLink
- And more

Selected Job Seeker Account Features:

- Include Job Seeker Badge on profile
- View salary details for LinkedIn job listings
- Move to the top of any job listing you apply for as a Featured Applicant
- See exactly who has viewed your profile
- InMail messaging opportunities
- LinkedIn webinar tips from top experts
- And more

EXPERT TIP

I personally have never upgraded my account before, but still have successfully managed to secure a full-time job and build an online brand community thanks to LinkedIn and the features its free account offers me.

Whether you're simply building your presence and network or actively seeking employment, think about what you can do for free on LinkedIn before pulling the trigger on a paid upgrade.

If your biggest career challenges can be solved with one or more features offered by a premium account, then by all means, upgrade.

However, you may find by seeking more LinkedIn advice on a specific challenge, you will achieve more success and can invest your money in other tools to advance your career.

AUTHOR:
Chris Perry

CHRIS PERRY

Chris Perry, MBA, is a Gen Y brand and marketing *generator*, career search and personal branding expert, professional speaker, entrepreneur and brand consultant.

Chris is the founder of **Career Rocketeer**, the Career Search and Personal Branding Network, as well as **MBA Highway**, the MBA Job Search and Career Network. He has multiple other ventures in the works.

His experience and advice have been featured in interviews, books, print publications and such media outlets as *The Wall Street Journal*, *SmartMoney*, ABCNews, CNNMoney, Inc.com, TheLadders.com, Monster.com and more.

Chris also offers career search and personal branding workshops and presentations to audiences of students and professionals.

Chris currently works full-time in CPG brand management and has worked on multiple brands across diverse industries.

Connect with the Generator:

- Personal Website: *http://www.chrisperry.me*
- Career Rocketeer: *http://www.careerrocketeer.com*
- MBA Highway: *http://www.mbahighway.com*

- LinkedIn: *http://www.linkedin.com/in/chrisaperry*
- Twitter: *http://twitter.com/careerrocketeer*
- Email: *careerrocketeer@gmail.com*

www.ingramcontent.com/pod-product-compliance
Lightning Source LLC
Chambersburg PA
CBHW060932050326
40689CB00013B/3059